Trucks, Trucks, Trucks by:

Kristi Cimbolic

And

Christopher J. Clarke

Trucks drive down the road.

Trucks can carry a heavy load.

Trucks can carry lots of cars.

Trucks can carry food really far.

Trucks can carry gas or oil.

Trucks can carry rocks or soil.

Trucks can carry bricks or logs.

Trucks can carry horses or hogs.

Trucks can carry milk or cheese.

Can I drive a truck please?

Parent/Teacher Guide

*use rhyming words to help read text:

road/load

car/far

oil/soil

log/hog

cheese/please

*use the story pattern to help read the text:

Trucks can carry_____.

*use the pictures to match the words: on page

one there is a picture of a truck so ask the

 reader what word he/she may see on the

 next page

*have children create some of their own pages

 using the pattern *trucks can carry_____.*

to make their own truck book

Dedicated to Stephen who loves trucks